D0461703

You Can Be a Gymnast

Alix Wood

Gareth Stevens
Publishing

Please visit our website, **www.garethstevens.com**. For a free color catalog of all our high-quality books, call toll free 1-800-542-2595 or fax 1-877-542-2596

Library of Congress Cataloging-in-Publication Data

Wood, Alix.
You can be a gymnast / by Alix Wood.
 p. cm. — (Let's get moving!)
Includes index.
ISBN 978-1-4824-0276-6 (pbk.)
ISBN 978-1-4824-0278-0 (6-pack)
ISBN 978-1-4824-0275-9 (library binding)
1. Gymnastics — Juvenile literature. I. Wood, Alix. II. Title.
GV461.3 W66 2014
796.44—dc23

First Edition

Published in 2014 by
Gareth Stevens Publishing
111 East 14th Street, Suite 349
New York, NY 10003

© Alix Wood Books

Produced for Gareth Stevens by Alix Wood Books
Designed by Alix Wood
Art direction and content research: Kevin Wood
Editor: Eloise Macgregor
Consultant: Mike Beagley, Falcons Gymnastics, Barnstaple, UK

Photo credits:
Cover, 1, 21 top, 24, 27 top and middle left © Shutterstock;
4 © Dmitry Berkut/Shutterstock; 22 top © muratart/Shutterstock;
all other photos © Chris Robbins

Acknowledgments
With grateful thanks to gymnasts Adam Tobin, Sophie Jeffery, Byron Day-Rogers, Daniel Mock, Ibrahim Kany, Joe Cemlyn-Jones, Phailin Ferracin and Ryan Owen

Printed in the United States of America

CPSIA compliance information: Batch # CW14GS: For further information contact Gareth Stevens, New York, New York at 1-800-542-2595.

All sports can be dangerous. Do not attempt any of the skills in this book without supervision from a trained adult expert.

Contents

Why Do Gymnastics?

Gymnastics is fun and keeps you fit. Doing gymnastics can help your self-confidence and get you strong and flexible.

There are so many ways you can enjoy gymnastics. There are five main types of gymnastics: artistic, **rhythmic**, trampolining, acrobatic, and **synchronized**. Artistic gymnastics is the one most people see on TV. It is divided into men's and women's. Men have six events, including the vault, pommel horse, parallel bars, high bar, rings, and floor. The women have four events—vault, bars, beam, and floor.

> Rhythmic gymnasts do dancelike routines with a ribbon, rope, hoop, club, or ball. Sometimes groups of rhythmic gymnasts do routines together.

Trampolining and tumbling involve moves on a trampoline, a mini-tramp, or tumbling on a special bouncy floor. Acrobatic gymnastics is a competitive partner sport where two or more gymnasts perform routines. Synchronized gymnastics involves a team of gymnasts typically either all men or all women.

Two acrobatic gymnasts practice their routine. These girls called this move the "superman!"

TRY THIS Most people who reach the top level of gymnastics start when they are very young. Don't let that put you off, though. You can start at any age. Contact a club near your home and see what classes they have that interest you.

Warming Up

Doing gymnastics can cause injuries. It is vital to do a good warm-up. A warm-up stretches your muscles and helps you to avoid injury.

A good warm-up should start with some **cardio** exercise, such as a 5-minute jog. Then you should warm up all the different parts of the body. Do arm circles to the front and back to warm up your shoulders. Gently stretch out your wrists and ankles, and turn your neck. Roll your ankles around to flex the joint. Make sure you stretch your hamstrings and calves well before you attempt an exercise such as the splits. Do the same gentle exercises to cool down after a gym session, too.

A gentle jog is one of the best warm-ups.

To stretch your hamstrings, arms, and calf muscles, try these exercises. With stretches it is important not to strain yourself. Stretch gently as far as you can without feeling any pain.

This hamstring stretch helps warm up your leg muscles. Squat down with your hands flat on the floor.

Lift up your back, keeping your hands on the floor. Don't worry if you can't put your hands flat.

Gently try this center split. Sit and straddle your legs as wide as is comfortable. Keep your legs straight and toes pointed. Lean forward keeping your back straight. Hold the stretch.

Floor Work

In gymnastics, the floor refers to a specially prepared exercise surface. In competitions, an event performed on the floor is called a floor exercise.

The men's floor routine consists of tumbling. It must contain both forward, sideways, and backward tumbling as well as a single leg or arm balance. The women's floor routine is performed to music and has gymnastic, acrobatic, and dance elements. In your routine you must show off your best moves in a very short amount of time.

It may take many months of practice to learn to do a full split like this one. Take it gradually.

TRY THIS

After a good warm-up and plenty of stretches, you could try to do the splits. Stand in a straddle position and gradually slide down as far as you can. Keep your back knee tucked in, not facing out to the side. Try staying in that position for around 30 seconds. Remember to cool down after the exercise, too.

Once you have practiced the splits on the floor, you can use it in your floor routine in other ways. In gymnastics clubs the floor is used to practice for moves to be done on other apparatus also.

When you become good at gymnastics, these are the kind of floor moves you can do!

The spring floor has springs or rubber foam and plywood, which makes the floor bouncy. It softens the impact of landings and lets the gymnast gain height when tumbling.

Simple Floor Gymnastics

Here are some floor work moves to try. If you get good, you could try them on the beam!

A headstand may seem simple, but it is important to get it to look strong, elegant, **symmetrical**, and steady. Make sure you practice on a cushioned floor, with someone to help hold your legs in case you wobble.

Kneel down. Place your head on the floor. You will balance on the front of your hairline.

Raise your bottom and walk your feet toward your hands. Raise your feet from the floor. Hold in a tuck position with your knees bent.

Straighten your legs. Keep them together, with your toes pointed toward the ceiling.

A bridge is another floor exercise that can be used in routines. It is useful as a warm-up exercise for your spine, too.

Lie flat on your back.

Bend your knees. Place your hands palm down by your ears. Your fingers should be pointing at your shoulders.

Take a deep breath. Push up with your arms and legs and arch your back. Bend your knees, and lower yourself gently back down.

TRY THIS

At first do a bridge on the balls of your feet. It's easier.

The Pommel

The pommel is a piece of equipment used by male gymnasts in competitions.

It takes a great deal of strength, **coordination**, and skill to perform moves on the pommel. There are some cool ways that gymnastics coaches teach students the skills. One of them involves a bucket! Putting the gymnast's feet in a bucket on a rope allows the gymnast to contentrate on learning the correct body position.

Using a bucket on a rope helps teach gymnasts how to do a circle.

The equipment the gymnast in this picture is using is called a mushroom. It is closer to the ground and has a larger surface to move around than the pommel, so it is good for beginners. Coaches will often draw a clock face in chalk on the floor and teach the student to change positions at the different numbers.

A gymnast doing a circle using a mushroom.

TRY THIS

Build up your arm muscles by practicing push-ups. Push-ups can be done anywhere there is a flat surface. Get on the floor and support yourself by your toes and arms. Place your hands under your shoulders. Keep your body straight and lower yourself until your chest nearly touches the floor. Breathe out as you push back to the start position.

Useful Exercises

While doing a pommel horse routine, the whole weight of your body is supported by your wrists.

Gymnasts will often wear wrist supports when they are working on the pommel. In a move such as the circle, below, your hands are constantly lifting up and down and changing position as you swing around the pommel. You also use your **core** muscles in your **torso** to keep your body straight. Your shoulder muscles are important, too.

As the gymnast's legs swing around he must lift each hand to allow them to pass, and shift his weight to the other hand. Timing is critical.

GYMNOVA

The best training for the pommel is by repeatedly doing lots of pommel exercises! At home you won't be able to practice using a pommel horse or mushroom, however. You can still do exercises to help you. Try this L-sit lift.

L-sit lifts are great for gymnastics core conditioning. Sit on the floor with your legs straight out in front. Make sure the area behind you is clear in case you fall backward. Place your hands on the floor, just in front of your hips. Your hands can be flat or on knuckles. They can also be forward, sideways, or backward. Press yourself up into an L-sit and hold it for a few seconds.

Once you have mastered the L-sit you could try a V hold. Try to lift your legs as high as possible. Keep your elbows straight.

TRY THIS

In the background of the picture on the left a gymnast is doing a manna. These are very difficult to do! Notice he has his hands facing in the other direction. Keep practicing your L-sits and V holds and you may build up to trying a manna.

Using the Bars

There are three types of bar used in gymnastics. The high bar and **parallel** bars are used by male gymnasts. The uneven or **asymmetric** bars are used by female gymnasts.

the uneven bars

Some gymnasts wear hand guards to help them grip the bars. There are several different ways of holding the bars. Pictured below is an overhand grip. If you turn one hand the other way around it is called a mixed grip. Both hands the other way around is called a reverse or underhand grip.

Hand guards give support and help gymnasts train for longer.

Gymnasts put chalk on their hands and on the apparatus.

Gymnasts chalk their hands to help remove perspiration and reduce slipping.

The high bar is one of the most exciting gymnastics events. Gymnasts perform giant swings and spectacular **dismounts** that can include multiple flips or twists. The bar is over 9 feet (2.78 m) off the ground. A controlled dismount from this height is very difficult to do. You can practice a controlled dismount by jumping off something low onto a mat.

1

Land with both feet at the same time. Bend your knees and sit back. Use your arms to steady yourself. Try not to take an extra step if you can.

2

When you feel you are steady, raise your arms and smile!

Parallel Bars

A competition parallel bars routine usually includes a swing above the bars, below the bars, and a skill that involves releasing and regrasping both bars.

The gymnast mounts the apparatus either from a springboard or the floor. The gymnast must do every move with precision. Routines are judged on skill difficulty and **execution**. Points are deducted for bent knees, flexed feet, spread legs, and hops on the dismount landing. Points are added for skill difficulty. A gymnast who makes a mistake during a routine of more challenging skills might score higher than a gymnast who performs a less challenging routine flawlessly.

These low parallel bars are useful to train on for moves done above the bars.

TRY THIS

A lot of local parks have a set of parallel bars. See if one near where you live has a set. Always practice with someone else. You can help each other get on and off safely.

Practicing a handstand on the floor will help build up your skill and get your muscles ready for the parallel bars. Practice against a wall at first and use mats.

Kick one leg up, then follow with the other leg. Keep your arms and legs straight, and your legs together. Point your toes toward the ceiling. Don't arch your back or bend at the hips. Push down through your palms so your shoulders and arms are fully extended, and your elbows are locked out.

Lift your arms up over your head. Lunge forward and place both hands in front of you on the floor, shoulder-width apart, a foot away from the wall. Keep your fingers spread out and facing forward.

a handstand on the parallel bars

Vaulting

A competition vault is all over in a few seconds. Packing all the gymnast's skill into that short space of time is the challenge. You have to get every part right.

A gymnast must run fast and explode off the springboard to get as much height and **rotation** as possible. When gymnasts first learn the vault they often slow their run when they approach the board. Practice helps them stop slowing down.

A good run up and strong jump from the board means the gymnast can fly through the air!

Practicing sprinting is a great way to improve your vaulting skills. Warm up by jogging for a few minutes and doing some stretches. Then sprint fast for a short distance. Make L shapes with your arms, and swing your arms forward and backward. This helps your speed. You can even just stand and do the arm movements at home. Your muscles will build up if you repeat the movements until you feel the burn.

A vault run up area is 82 feet (25 m) long. You can choose how long your run up is. At the end of the run, the gymnast jumps onto the springboard.

1

The vault is 4.5 feet (1.35 m) high for men and 4.3 feet (1.25 m) high for women.

2

When you are starting out, try jumping onto the vault.

Then jump off. Remember to bend your knees when you land to absorb the fall.

The Beam

When you are performing on a 4-inch (10 cm) narrow beam, there is no room for mistakes.

Gymnasts practice on the floor and a low beam first. Once they can do a move well there, they move up to the high beam. Even something simple takes practice before you can perfect the skill on the beam. Gymnasts will have a spotter to help them. A spotter is a person, often your gymnastics coach, who stands ready to catch you if you fall.

Try this straddle L-sit. Sit in a straddle, with your legs straight and apart. Lean forward with your shoulders over your hands. Try to lift your heels off the ground.

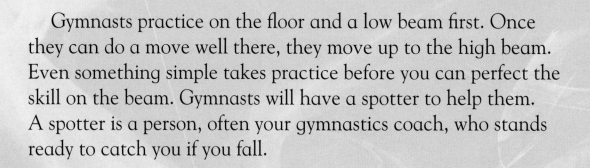

Once you have perfected the move on the floor, try it on a low beam and then a high beam.

Try perfecting this cartwheel on the floor, first.

Start your cartwheel with your arm that is on the same side as your front foot. Place your other arm a shoulder length further down the line.

Imagine a straight line on the ground. With both feet along the line, look at the point ahead where you will place your hands.

TRY THIS

The order goes: one arm down, opposite leg up, other arm down, opposite leg up.

While upside-down, look at your hands. This will help your balance. Land one foot, then the other. Straighten up.

Rings

Gymnasts perform moves from two rings which hang from a rigid metal frame. Only men compete in rings as it needs a lot of upper body strength.

The gymnast must use their strength to keep tension on the rings.

This L-sit is a static strength hold. It takes strength to keep still and stop the straps from wobbling.

Gymnasts need to have very strong arm muscles before they are allowed to use the rings. A good swing on the rings is harder than on the high bar. Gymnasts do swing, strength, and hold elements in their rings exercises. They usually include a swing to held handstand, a static strength hold, and an aerial dismount. In competitions, gymnasts are penalized for having bent arms in strength elements, or using the straps to support or balance themselves. There are also deductions if the cables swing a lot during a routine.

1

2

The rings are a long way up. Your coach may have to help you to grab hold of them.

You may need to use handgrips on the rings. Make sure you have mats underneath you.

3

4

You can try and pull yourself up into an L-sit. Have a spotter help you.

When you get good, you can try to lift your hips over your head. Your spotter should help hold you.

Trampoline

Trampolining develops air sense, spatial awareness, and strength. It is a competitive Olympic sport. Gymnasts perform routines while bouncing on a trampoline.

There are some important safety measures to understand before you begin to trampoline. Trampolining should always be supervised. Never trampoline alone. It is very easy to hurt yourself. It is a good idea to wear socks. This stops your toes from entering any gaps in the trampoline webbing.

A trampoline move in a tucked position

TRY THIS

In competitions, moves are usually performed in one of the following three basic shapes:

tucked with knees clasped to chest by hands

piked with hands touching close to feet and both arms and legs straight

straddle legs creating a triangle with hands on ankles

Competitive trampolining routines consist of combinations of 10 contacts with the trampoline bed. You need to learn to land in four positions—feet, seat, front, and back. A routine must always start and finish on your feet.

To do a pike, jump up with your hands raised above your head. Keep your legs together and straight.

Bring your arms down and forward, and touch your feet. Hold your stomach in. Slide your hands back along your legs and to the side of your body until you land on your feet.

A safe foam area surrounds this gym's trampoline.

Acrobatic

Acrobatic gymnastics, or acro, is a partner sport. Each pair or group competes in three routines to test their balance, power, and skills.

This move is most definitely not for beginners! The stand on shoulders is a great acro move. It must only be learned with correct instruction, at a gym, and with spotters and safety mats. Do not try this at home.

The girls join hands in a cross grip. Girl A is on the left. Girl B is on the right.

Girl B semi-squats. Girl A places her right foot on Girl B's thigh. They join both hands.

3

Girl A steps up, using downward arm pressure to help lift herself. She turns around and places her left foot on Girl B's shoulder.

5

When Girl A is steady, Girl B shifts her grip to Girl A's calves. Girl A extends her arms.

Only practice this move with an instructor and with a spotter who can catch you if you start to fall.

4

Holding both hands to steady herself, Girl A stands up.

TRY THIS

Join a gymnastics club to see if you like it. It's a great way to challenge yourself.

Glossary

asymmetric Not identical on both sides of a central line; lacking symmetry.

cardio Concerning the heart.

coordination Smooth working together, such as good muscular coordination.

core The deep muscles in the torso.

dismounts The action of getting down from something.

execution Carrying through something to its finish.

flexible Capable of being bent.

parallel Lying or moving in the same direction but always the same distance apart.

rhythmic Of, relating to, or having rhythm.

rotation The act of rotating, especially on an axis.

spatial awareness The ability to be aware of oneself in space.

symmetrical Having, involving, or showing symmetry, which is a close agreement in size, shape, and relative position.

synchronized Occurring or operating at the same time or rate.

torso The trunk of the human body.

For More Information

Books

Savage, Jeff. *Top 25 Gymnastics Skills, Tips, and Tricks.* Berleley Heights, NJ: Enslow Pubishers Inc., 2012.

Schlegel, Elfi. *The Gymnastics Book: The Young Performer's Guide to Gymnastics.* Buffalo, NY: Firefly Books, 2012.

Websites

Gymnastics Technique and Training
www.drillsandskills.com
Visit a forum for gymnasts, coaches, or anyone who just wants to learn about gymnastics skills.

It's My Life
pbskids.org/itsmylife/body/teamsports/article8.html
Information, advice, and links about gymnastics are found here.

Teens Health
kidshealth.org/teen/safety/sports_safety/safety_gymnastics.html
Get some advice about gymnastics safety.

Publisher's note to educators and parents: Our editors have carefully reviewed these websites to ensure that they are suitable for students. Many websites change frequently, however, and we cannot guarantee that a site's future contents will continue to meet our high standards of quality and educational value. Be advised that students should be closely supervised whenever they access the Internet.

Index